LIVING IN LOVE

A 40-DAY DEVOTIONAL

Jay Haizlip

Copyright © 2014 by Jay Haizlip. All rights reserved.

All rights reserved. No part of this publication may be reproduced, distributed, or transmitted in any form or by any means, including photocopying, recording, or other electronic or mechanical methods, without the prior written permission of the publisher, except in the case of brief quotations embodied in critical reviews and certain other noncommercial uses permitted by copyright law. For permission requests, write to the publisher, addressed "Attention: Permissions Coordinator," at the address below.

Fedd Books
P.O. Box 341973
Austin, TX 78734
www.thefeddagency.com

Published in association with the literary and entertainment agency, The Fedd Agency, Inc.

Book design by Mitchell Shea
Book production by Fedd Books, www.thefeddagency.com
Editing by Cara Highsmith, www.highsmithcreativeservices.com

Translation:
Unless otherwise indicated, all scripture comes from the NKJV translation.

"Scripture taken from the New King James Version®. Copyright © 1982 by Thomas Nelson, Inc. Used by permission. All rights reserved."

Scripture quotations marked (NLT) are taken from the Holy Bible, New Living Translation, copyright © 1996, 2004, 2007 by Tyndale House Foundation. Used by permission of Tyndale House Publishers, Inc., Carol Stream, Illinois 60188. All rights reserved.

Printed in the United States of America
First Printing, 2014
ISBN paperback: 978-0-9907044-1-6
ISBN Ebook: 978-0-9907044-2-3

Categories: Religion: Inspirational, Religion:Devotional, Religion: Christianity

Contents

Introduction

Falling in Love   1

Being Fearless in Love   43

Being Limitless in Love   85

Living in Love   127

INTRODUCTION

That their hearts may be encouraged, being knit together in love, and attaining to all riches of the full assurance of understanding, to the knowledge of the mystery of God, both of the Father and of Christ...
—Colossians 2:2

If you were to ask me what one topic is most on my heart as I speak and minister, I would have to say it is "love." Now, I know that sounds like a really broad subject and it could mean a lot of things. That's true because it covers a lot of ground. In fact, there are so many different kinds of love—brotherly love, romantic love, family love, and godly love—and so many ways people express it that it can be hard to know what someone is really saying when they use the word *love*. But even with all of those possibilities, this one thing is true: love is the root that connects us.

In 1 John 4:16, the Bible says, "We have known and

believed the love that God has for us. God is love, and he who abides in love abides in God, and God in him." This verse speaks to my heart because I believe God has called me to share His love with the world and show others what it means to put love on and live in it and begin to live in God as well.

We all want to receive love and know as Christians we are called to give love even when it isn't easy. This 40-Day Devotional is broken into four sections that will walk you through the tough parts of experiencing and sharing in authentic love. Section 1, "Falling in Love," begins with why we love and why we need to love better. Section 2 is called "Being Fearless in Love" and covers all the different issues people come up against when they try to love that stand in the way of doing it effectively. The focus of Section 3 is "Becoming Limitless in Love." This is where we discover the potential of love and how far it can go. The last section goes deeper to "Living in Love" and we begin to understand what it means to live in love and make that our focus. At the end of each devotion I have included space for you to write down your thoughts about the message, a prayer for yourself and others, or maybe steps you can take to really begin living in love. I hope you will use that to go further in understanding what God wants to teach you about His love.

I know there are thousands of devotionals you could use in your daily study, and I bet a lot of them are on the topic of love. With so much out there, I want to say I appreciate your choosing *Living in Love* and if you take away only one thing from this devotional, I hope it will be a clearer sense of how much God loves you and how transformative love can be.

I pray that you will have an encounter with love that changes who you are and everything you do so you can truly live love.

Pastor Jay

Section 1
FALLING IN LOVE

DAY 1
In Love Everything Begins

And the Word became flesh and dwelt among us, and we beheld His glory, the glory as of the only begotten of the Father, full of grace and truth.

—John 1:14

The one thing we all have in common as human beings is the need for love—to give it and receive it. But we can have a hard time understanding what love is really supposed to look like because of past experiences with love not done the right way.

When we get hung up on what has gone wrong it is important to go back to the root, the foundation of what love really is and what it is all about. Although it might be an instinct to want love, we need to understand why we are drawn to it.

John 1:14 tells us about Jesus caoming to walk among us. God sent His son to show us the way to grow closer to Him and to live in Him because of His love for us.

We can also turn to John 1:1, which tells us, "In the beginning was the Word, and the Word was with God, and the Word was God." That means that if Jesus is the Word, being full of love, and He was at the beginning of everything, then love must be the beginning of everything.

Even though it can be hard to see sometimes, love was at the center of God's desire to make all of creation. He wanted to be able to give abundant love and have a relationship with us. Can you imagine what a great thing it is to be so loved by someone that they would create life just for you, just so you could exist for them to love you?

If we take this same approach in our lives and start with love in everything we do, we can't help but find the joy that comes from being in God and being aligned with God.

If you can start your day loving the fact that you

have a new chance to grow in love and discover more about God and who He wants you to be, you will find it much easier to deal with anything that comes up. That makes it possible to work through your day loving how God is teaching you through everything you experience. And, you can end your day loving the fact that God brought you through another twenty-four hours safely and with great blessings.

When we learn how to live in love, we are able to place love at the beginning of everything we do, think, and feel. With that as our foundation, great things are bound to happen!

LIVING IN LOVE: As you go through your day today, try to treat every encounter, even with the most difficult person you meet, as an opportunity to love.

DAY 2
In Love There Is Truth

By this we know love, because He laid down His life for us. And we also ought to lay down our lives for the brethren.

—1 John 3:16

One of the hardest parts about releasing ourselves to love is understanding what real love looks like and being able to trust that we can know it when we see it. Many times we are afraid to give love because we have been deceived in the past or were mistreated when we tried to love someone. Sometimes we thought we were getting love in return that turned out to be a lie.

But, in love there is truth. When we are looking to the example Jesus set for us through His life, we can know how real love looks and acts. We have a guide for how real love treats others and the motives it has for every word and action. All we have to do is follow Jesus' example.

Jesus showed us that real love is sacrificial. Yes, 1 John 3:16 talks about giving up your life for someone you love. Most of us have a hard time thinking about going that far, and hopefully we won't ever have to face that choice; but, Jesus made smaller sacrifices throughout His ministry that we can follow too. He gave up His pride and His position in Heaven to serve us. He let go of His need to be admired to be able to speak truth to those in power who didn't like what He had to say.

Jesus showed us that real love is kind. He was tender and generous with His heart and spirit. Jesus chose to reach out to and spend time with the people in the community who were considered outcasts— the children, the morally and physically unclean, the poor and needy. He didn't avoid people who were unpleasant, but sought them out just so He could love them.

Jesus showed us that real love is patient. He did not get angry easily, and He took the time to explain where someone had gone wrong and led them back to the path of righteousness. Even though He knew His time with us was limited, He was careful not to make people feel shamed into following Him. He loved them to the place that they chose Him.

Jesus showed us that real love is eternal. Though He was only on Earth for a short time, Jesus brought a love that would last through the ages. He gave us a love that would carry us to eternity where we could be with Him.

These are the truths we find in love and the example we can use as we learn how to give and receive authentic love. We can become sacrificial, kind, and patient as we love others and can expect that out of the love we get in return. This is what helps us learn to live in love.

LIVING IN LOVE: Take a look at the truth of how you love and apply the standards Jesus set. Begin working to reflect His way of loving.

DAY 3
In Love There Are No Questions

Behold what manner of love the Father has bestowed on us, that we should be called children of God! Therefore the world does not know us, because it did not know Him.

—1 John 3:1

The doubt and insecurity we feel when we encounter love most often come from not really understanding the nature of love. Too many of us have had experiences where we were not loved right by someone who was supposed to love us or where we have let down someone we were supposed to love. Those disappointments distort our perception of what we think we can expect out of love.

The questions that come up can keep us from even giving love a chance to be something good in our lives. We wonder, *Why do you love me? What is it about me that makes you love me?* We need reasons for why God would even give us a second thought, much less pursue us with love.

We investigate every angle looking for some devious motive or agenda. We are suspicious of every word and action, and it keeps us completely distanced from the love we need. It can be really hard to let go of the past that influences how we relate to love because it calls for trust in something we can't see. But, there is plenty of proof available to give us confidence in what God wants us to have.

Here is the only evidence you need: God doesn't ask anything in return for His love. We are His creation and He made us to love us. God doesn't need a reason for His love. We are His children and He just wants to love us. We are His and He is going to love us even if we don't love Him back.

This no-strings-attached kind of love is not easy for us to accept because we keep looking at it from the perspective of what we have experienced in the past and what we think we are capable of on our own. As long as we use that to measure God's love, it will always come up short. But God is so much bigger than that. So, when we ask, *Why do you love me?* He answers, *Because I do.* When we ask, *What is it about me that makes you love me?* He answers, *Because I made you.*

Then God asks us, *I made you specifically to be who you are, so why wouldn't I love you as you are? I made you because I wanted to know you, so why wouldn't I love who you are?* Let these responses remove all doubt that God is passionately and fervently longing to love you. As you start to embrace the love of God, if you still have questions, let them be, *How far can I spread the love God has shown me? Who in my life hasn't yet learned how deep the love of God goes? How much more can I do in my life with God's love as my guide?*

LIVING IN LOVE: Our questions get in the way of love, so stop letting them talk you out of the love God wants you to have.

DAY 4
In Love There Is No Past

Let *love* be *without hypocrisy. Abhor what is evil. Cling to what is good.*

—Romans 12:9

We looked at the questions that come up as a result of our pasts and how they can affect our perspectives on love. The truth is, our choices, disappointments, failures, fears, and other life-changing experiences impact more than just the ability to receive and give love. They can skew our view of whether we even deserve love and make us question if we can truly love someone else.

We all carry our pasts with us into the present and the future, and that won't change. They are as much a part of us as our fingerprints. But, when you really begin to comprehend God's love, you learn that even though you have a past, and even if parts of it may haunt you, they don't matter a single bit to God. He couldn't care less about what you did, and he certainly doesn't want to hang on to what anyone else did to you in your past. That means your past doesn't have to keep having a negative effect on your life. You have a chance to release it and have a new way of living.

Those old mistakes and wounds are washed away in the cleansing power of God's perfect love. The hurt and embarrassment of your past don't have a place in your present because He is healing you. All of the things that made you feel unloved, unworthy of love, or incapable of love will fall away when you let God show you how much He loves you and that it has nothing to do with how good or how deserving you are.

God does not keep a tally of your "obedience" deposits to see if you've racked up enough credit to earn some of His love. He doesn't have a scorecard to track how many points you earn by your good deeds or your "pay it forward" actions. And He definitely doesn't save His love for people who are perfect. If He operated that way, we would be in the negative before we hit preschool, so there is no way to work off that deficit. God just loves us anyway.

It is so hard to let go of the past and move forward, but that is what God's love allows us to do. Can you imagine making a conscious choice to hold tightly to all the stuff that hurt you or someone else in your life? Can you imagine thinking being stuck is better than being free of that baggage? Yet, that is exactly what we are doing when we refuse to accept the love God wants to give us, and we end up missing out on all He has in store for us.

How great is it that your past is a blank slate as far as God is concerned? Even the ways someone mistreated you can be wiped away with the love of God so you don't have to live in that pain. You get to live in love.

LIVING IN LOVE: Stop clinging to your past and make a commitment to yourself that when God removes the pain of the past, you won't go looking for it.

DAY 5
In Love There Is God

He who does not love does not know God, for God is love.

—1 John 4:8

It's a pretty powerful statement to say that those who don't love don't know God. It's also going to confuse a lot of people. We all like to think we love and love well. We love our parents, our spouses, our children, our friends. Why is that so hard? We can even say we love that person in church who gossips or the co-worker who tries to be the boss even when they aren't in charge. Around the holidays we even love those who are less fortunate. But is that the kind of love God is talking about in the Bible?

Oftentimes we get too comfortable with the word *love* to such an extent that we say we *LOVE* a particular flavor of ice cream; we *LOVE* our favorite sports team;

we *LOVE* an actress on TV; and we *LOVE* the weekends. But, this really isn't love. It would be more accurate to say we crave that ice cream, we support our teams, we admire the actress, and we enjoy our weekends. When we use "love" to describe how we feel about the less important things in life, it loses some of its significance for the bigger things.

We can get used to love being something that is superficial and temporary, so it's no wonder we get mixed up and have a hard time understanding love so deep, so intimate, and so unwavering that it goes beyond all we can imagine. Real love—God's love—is so much more than affection or appreciation, and He sent Jesus to show us what that looks like.

When we have the kind of love that shows we know God, we put the needs of others before our own. Really loving means forgetting about past wrongs and forgiving. True love is accepting someone's faults and flaws and loving all of them unconditionally. When we are able to give this kind of love, we show God that we understand His heart and the instruction He gave us through Jesus' example.

John 13:35 says, "By this all will know that you are My disciples, if you have love for one another." Along with 1 John 4:8, God is showing us in His word that He is at the center of all the love we will experience or share with others. We can't truly know God and not love, and when we truly love, others can't help but see God in us.

It is true that we might be able to experience some level of love without God in our lives, but it is nothing compared to the kind of love we will know in Him.

LIVING IN LOVE: Make the choice to know God and receive His love so others will see Him in you. Do your best each day to show someone how much God loves them.

DAY 6
In Love There Is Simplicity

He chose us in Him before the foundation of the world, that we should be holy and without blame before Him in love.

—Ephesians 1:4

One of the biggest reasons we struggle to understand God's love is that a love that big just doesn't make sense to us. We look for explanations of why He would love us when we feel unlovable. We question whether this kind of love is for real or if it is just some overblown promise that can't be fulfilled. We are suspicious of the hidden motives when there doesn't seem to be any price we have to pay for it. We overcomplicate something that is very simple.

Just as Paul wrote in Ephesians, God chose us before He even began making a world. He wanted us and He wanted to love us. He chose to love us just because. There is no need to dig through scripture or pray for Him to reveal His reasons because the answer will be the same over and over. He loves us because He loves us. It's that simple.

Now, just because something is simple, that doesn't mean it's going to be a piece of cake. We run into lots of obstacles with simple concepts because we overthink them. We struggle with understanding God's love because we think there have to be certain conditions attached to receiving love. Being able to take on faith that God loves us for no other reason than because He wants to is a lot to accept when you aren't used to getting something for nothing.

One of the hardest things for us to do when we have not been loved right or have never learned how to love someone else is to believe that someone out there wants to love us purely and simply because He can and that this love isn't going to change on a whim.

But simple doesn't mean easy. Simple can actually be one of the hardest things you are faced with in life.

But, man, what a great thing it is when we get it. It all clicks. It all makes sense in a way that no one can make you question it ever again.

Simplicity can be a blessing and a curse. It is a curse because being able to find the faith to trust something so simple is hard to do. That's especially true when you have a tendency to think too much and get stuck in your head about something that is going on in your heart. But, simplicity is also a blessing when you allow it to strip away all the excuses and objections so you can just know the simple but pure and lasting love of God. Simplicity—that's what we have in God's love, and that is the kind of clarity we get when we live in love.

LIVING IN LOVE: Follow the old acronym K.I.S.S.—Keep It Simple Stupid. Don't make God's love more complicated than it is.

DAY 7
In Love There Is Direction

A new commandment I give to you, that you love one another; as I have loved you, that you also love one another.

—John 13:34

When Jesus came to walk and live among us, the world had been caught up in religiosity—all the dos and don'ts, all the rules and regulations—and had become lost. They were focused on all of the sacrifices and other rituals that would keep them in good with God. Their relationship with God was completely works-based, and the more time that passed, the more conditions and expectations there were placed on pleasing God and keeping Him happy.

When Jesus came, this group of people not only had the 10 Commandments, they had hundreds of other laws—Levitical laws—that gave them rules on what kinds of fibers they could mix, which foods could be eaten which ways, and how to wear their hair. They had all of this instruction, but they had no direction. They had been wandering away from and back to God off and on for centuries.

But, Jesus told these rule-followers, "I have a new commandment. I want you to love one another. Don't love the laws, because that is not what is going to show others that you love me and follow me. That is not what will glorify God." These people who were so obsessed with all the stuff they could do to get God to love them were just told that none of it mattered and that loving others the way God loved them was the path to what they were seeking. That must have been confusing, alarming, and freeing all at the same time.

Can you imagine being told you didn't have to jump through a bunch of hoops and could skip a whole lot of steps to get to your end goal? It sounds great, and I think we'd all like to have someone tell us that at work, in school, and other areas of life, but think about how you might feel if you counted on the rules to show you how to think, how to act, how to live? They must have felt like the rug was pulled out from under them.

What they didn't realize until later is that they were released to a freedom they had never known before and that removing all of those other guidelines would allow God to come in and personally direct their lives. Jesus gave us the most basic instruction—love one another as I have loved you—and that brings a new direction to a richer life and a deeper relationship with God and the people in our lives.

LIVING IN LOVE: "Love one another" is the only rule you need. As you learn to live in love, let that guide how you conduct yourself in every other area of life, and begin to make better choices as you take that direction.

DAY 8
In Love We Are Complete

"May [you] be able to comprehend with all the saints what is the width and length and depth and height—to know the love of Christ which passes knowledge; that you may be filled with all the fullness of God.
—Ephesians 3:18-19

Too often in our lives we choose to close ourselves off from love because we have been disappointed by it in the past. We harden our hearts and shut ourselves down in the hopes that we will protect ourselves from being hurt again. From a defense standpoint, that makes a lot of sense. If you are vulnerable and susceptible to attack, you build up better walls and barricades.

The only problem with that is we weren't meant to live behind a fortress. We weren't meant to hide from personal relationships. God made us to embody

His love and to reflect His love to the rest of the world. We are not fulfilling our purposes when we refuse to let love into our lives or allow it to flow through us to others.

If you've been overprotective of your heart and have taken extra precautions in who you let close to you, you probably also feel a big, gaping hole in your life. You may not have recognized it yet or may be choosing to ignore it, but you are incomplete if you are guarding yourself against love.

God designed us with a need for love so we would pursue Him and want to share Him with everyone we meet. When we aren't letting that love in, there is a big component of who we are that is missing. In love we find our calling; in love we find meaning; in love we find wholeness.

If you've been holding back from loving someone or letting someone love you because you are afraid of being hurt or disappointed, think about how much you are really suffering by not being completely who you were made to be. Think about what it means to go through life with a piece of you missing. Isn't it worth the risk to be able to finally know that every part of you is fully connected and functioning the way it should? Isn't it worth letting down your guard so you can give God room to enter your heart?

When we fully comprehend the love God has for us, we discover that it goes beyond anything we've experienced before. When we understand just how incredible His love is, we don't run from it. We run to love. The walls and barricades crumble, and we step into the complete love of God and the complete life He planned for us. We become complete.

Let God show you what life can be like when you open yourself fully to receiving and giving love. Stop building walls that keep you disconnected from your purpose. Discover the whole person you will become when you live in love.

LIVING IN LOVE: Take the necessary steps and open yourself up to receiving the love that God wants to pour into your life. Allow love to flow through you and out to the world.

DAY 9
In Love There Are Benefits

"Father, I desire that they also whom You gave Me may be with Me where I am, that they may behold My glory which You have given Me; for You loved Me before the foundation of the world."

—John 17:24

We've talked about how living in love offers truth and removes all the doubts and questions that keep us from trusting. We've gone over the ways it is a simple and clear choice. But, if finding God and the wholeness His love brings to your life is not enough reason to choose to live love, let me tell you about the other benefits.

Maybe you've heard the verse, 1 John 2:3, "Now by this we know that we know Him, if we keep His commandments." And, maybe you think that to be able to really love God you have to keep His commandments first. But, that's not what that verse says. What it really says is people will be able to tell that you love God, and God will know you love Him when you are keeping his commandments. That means that loving God makes you want to follow His commandments.

Religion may tell you that you have to be holy or set aside to know God. I'm here to tell you, it is *impossible* for us to get holy and right with God without knowing Him first. The fruit of knowing God is becoming holy. The kind of sanctification religion wants you to have is not something you can accomplish on your own. Otherwise we wouldn't need Jesus.

Another benefit I want you to know about—and probably the most important one for any of us—is the reward of eternity. Knowing God's love in this life is important because it changes you and your experiences. Having a relationship with Him guides you through the tough choices, the fear and uncertainty, and the heartaches of life. But, the endgame and the ultimate purpose of why we are here is not to suffer through human life and then be done. It's to go on to be with God in Heaven where we get to experience the fullness of His love in a way that is not affected by the limitations of the flesh.

What we begin to experience when we choose to live in love is nothing compared to what is waiting for us when we are invited into God's presence in Heaven. What reason on Earth can you think of for turning that down? What in this world is better than knowing you get to be with God after you die?

They say membership has its privileges. And, the benefit of choosing to live in love is that this club is not exclusive and there is no trial or probationary period. The moment you decide you want a relationship with God, you're in, and the perks just keep getting better.

LIVING IN LOVE: Start discovering the best part of God's love. Embrace the benefits that come from knowing Him more intimately, and let it spark a fire in you for pursuing His heart with everything you have.

DAY 10
In Love You Are His

For God is not unjust to forget your work and labor of love which you have shown toward His name, in that you have ministered to the saints, and do minister.
—Hebrews 6:10

Let's go back to that verse in John 13:35, "By this all will know that you are My disciples, if you have love for one another." We looked at how it proves to us that God is at the center of love. Now I want to use it to show you how it sets us apart us in a special category. That means they will identify us as belonging to God, as being followers of Jesus.

When we love the way God loves us, God aligns Himself with us and begins to fill us with His love to the point that it is overflowing. When we let that spill over onto everyone around us, there is a unique character and countenance we carry. What people start to see is

God in us and they identify us with Him. We are known as His.

Sometimes it makes people uncomfortable to encounter someone who clearly belongs to God. Seeing another person so full of the love of God shines a big, bright spotlight on what is missing in their own lives. We might meet with resistance to the love we want to share. *Oh, I don't need that. I'm just fine as I am.* We might hear negative comments or criticism. *Why do you have to go around telling everyone about this? Can't you just keep it to yourself?* We might get a judgmental response. *How can you believe in that? You're a fool to buy into that fantasy.*

But, it doesn't matter what anyone else thinks. It matters what God thinks, and if He is looking down on you in love and saying, "See him right there? See her over there? They are mine! I love them and I am proud of them!," then every other opinion is irrelevant. If He has called you His, you can deal with any other name-calling you might encounter.

Living in love means you get to walk through life with the love of God wrapped tightly around you as comfort and as protection from any enemy who would rise up against you. We all want to be loved and belong to someone. When you know God, you will know the greatest love you'll ever find, and you belong to the only one who really matters. Isn't it time you turned your heart over to Him? Isn't it time you let Him love you the way you deserve to be loved?

LIVING IN LOVE: Allow yourself to be claimed by God; take that big step in discovering who you really are in Him. Live in that kind of love and open up your world to brothers and sisters who will support you in the journey.

Section 2

BEING FEARLESS IN LOVE

DAY 11
In Love There Are No Judgments

With all lowliness and gentleness, with longsuffering, [bear] with one another in love.

—Ephesians 4:2

I can't think of a bigger challenge to our ability to love and be loved than our tendency to cast judgment. In fact, the church has a big PR problem because we preach love but don't really manage to get that message across through our actions.

How many times have you heard someone say, "I don't want anything to do with Christians; You are all so judgmental; All you want to do is fix what you think is wrong with me"? How many times have you been the one saying these things? When Jesus left the earth, his instruction was to love each other and to go out and be His representatives. He wanted us to keep modeling the example he set for us and show each other kindness and acceptance. He loved everyone without judgment and He didn't hold back from anyone. But, in His name, the love we dole out has all kinds of conditions and expectations.

Even the practices we think are a reflection of love and concern can be seen as judgmental. "I haven't seen you in church lately. Where have you been?" or "Why are you friends with that person? They are going to be a bad influence." And, that's just within the church family. To outsiders we say, "You've got to get right with Jesus," or "Your life is a mess. You need God."

The message of love would come through so much more quickly if we said, "We miss your presence when you are gone. I hope you can come back soon," or "I'm glad you are spending time with that person and loving on them." We should be opening our arms and our hearts to everyone we meet, saying, "I want you to know how much Jesus loves you," or "Let me share God's love with you. What do you need to make your life better? How can I help?"

In many cases, judgmental attitudes come from our own fears of being judged on the way we dress, the way we act, or the way we live. We have come to expect that out of life. If we can break this cycle and stop a judgmental thought before it takes shape, we stand a much better chance of being able to love others unconditionally—the way God wants us to love.

Judgment is not in love. It only stands in the way of love. Whether you are the one judging or the one feeling judged, this is a barrier that does not reflect the way God wants us to love and definitely does not resemble the love He has for us. Drawing closer to that unconditional love He has for you will help you to learn how to give that kind of love to everyone else you meet.

LIVING IN LOVE: Pay attention to judgmental thoughts as the come up, and try to turn that thought into one that is love-oriented instead.

DAY 12
In Love There Is No Rejection

Who shall separate us from the love of Christ? Shall tribulation, or distress, or persecution, or famine, or nakedness, or peril, or sword?

—Romans 8:35

One of the ways our past experiences really mess with our view of love is in creating this deeply rooted fear of rejection. We have become so used to this happening that we automatically assume rejection will be a part of any relationship that involves love. It may not happen right away—in fact, we might get lured in to love under false pretenses and think they have accepted us, only to have it fall apart after we have gotten comfortable. Other times we are rejected from the beginning based on some superficial judgment and feel we won't ever be loved because no one can get past that initial impression.

These fears lead to feelings of being inadequate, of being unworthy or unwanted. They keep us feeling that we don't deserve any kind of love, and especially the love God has for us. But, God's love is the most accepting and open love there is. He wants everyone to receive His love. He wants everyone to know Him and know His love, no matter what kind of past they have and no matter what kind of life they are living now. And, He won't revoke his love because of something you say or do later. It's a no-strings-attached kind of love and it isn't going away.

Regardless of what your fears might tell you or what you've experienced in the past, God's love is not a works-based kind of relationship. You cannot mess up or slip up and lose His love. You don't have to worry that if your performance each day doesn't measure up that God isn't going to love you that day. His love is consistent and unwavering.

It can be hard to grasp that kind of love, but we experience it on some level when we have children.

For most of us, we can't imagine anything our sons or daughters could do that would make us stop loving them. We might not like what they do; we might be deeply disappointed in them; we might even have to cut off our support of them; but we never stop loving them. That is the kind of love God has for us, but on a God-sized level.

Rejection is a big fear for all of us, even if we try to pretend it isn't. However, we also know that if we don't take the risk of rejection, we never get to any of the rewards that are waiting. God's love is the biggest payoff, and for the smallest risk because His love is the one sure thing we can count on.

LIVING IN LOVE: Give yourself a chance to experience the love of God and find out for yourself that there is no rejection in pure love.

DAY 13
In Love There Is No Torment

There is no fear in love; but perfect love casts out fear, because fear involves torment. But he who fears has not been made perfect in love.

—1 John 4:18

Isn't it tormenting to think the love available to you is based on how well you perform on a particular day and that you could lose that love if you don't act or live exactly how someone else wants you to? When you believe that love is a works-based relationship, living with the fear of judgment and rejection is part of your daily life. But that isn't all. You live with the torment of constantly questioning yourself and your abilities, worrying that even when you do your best it will never be enough.

You may also begin to wonder if nothing you do matters and think the love can be taken away just because the other person decides not to give it anymore through no fault of your own. Isn't it tormenting to think that you are not really free in that relationship? That is not how love is supposed to feel. Torment is not a part of perfect love.

Now, the opposite of torment is comfort. And we can find comfort in knowing that God's love is bigger than all of us and all of our human limitations. In Ephesians 3:16 and 19, Paul explains that the love of God is a supernatural thing that we have to perceive because we can never understand the God kind of love on a natural level. It has to happen in the spirit. When you get a revelation of the fact that you are loved and that He has a purpose for your life, you have the comforting knowledge of the width and length and depth and height of God's love.

While the torment we experience in love can be at the hands of someone who is cruel and heartless, who rejects us and takes advantage of our love, we often have greater torment that is self-inflicted. We hang on to old wounds and we guard against healing love because we fear it will be the same hurtful experience all over again. We stay stuck feeling miserable because we think that is what we deserve.

Perfect love lifts the torment and brings comfort to our aching hearts and souls by revealing to us the love that passes all understanding. God can show you the depth of His love if you open your heart to Him and release yourself from the torment of your past.

LIVING IN LOVE: Give yourself permission to release the tormenting experiences of your past so God's perfect love can make you whole.

DAY 14
In Love There Are No Rules and Regulations

For when we place our faith in Christ Jesus ... what is important is faith expressing itself in love.

—Galatians 5:6 [NLT]

Many of us refuse to embrace God's love because we believe there are long lists of conditions that go along with it. The Dos and Don'ts that we think we have to follow to receive His love make us feel like maybe it just isn't worth it. The possibility for slipping up seems too big and we decide to skip the hassle.

Those who feel this way have good reason. Whether they grew up in church or not, most people are familiar with the Ten Commandments and all the other things the Bible says we should or shouldn't do. But, what they don't understand is that not one of these rules and regulations has anything to do with God's love or our worthiness to receive it.

I don't want you to get the idea that the things God laid out in His word for how He wants us to live don't matter. They are important; but they don't win you God's love or help you keep it. God loves you—plain and simple. There is not a thing you can do to improve your chances with Him or cause Him to decide you aren't worth the hassle for Him. He has loved you from the beginning when He first thought of creating you, and He will love you through every breath you take, every thought you have, and every choice you make to the very end of time. But, when you love God and are growing closer to Him, the things He laid out in the Bible become more important to you, and you will begin to choose to live according to those guidelines.

See, God knows what has happened in the past, what is happening now, and what will happen in the future, so He has a perspective on every single life that none of us can have. He sees the whole picture and that is why He said there are certain types of behaviors, certain ways of living that we should avoid. He knows the kind of heartache and struggle those choices will bring us down the road, and He is trying to direct us away from them. It isn't about restricting our ability to enjoy life. It's about helping us find out how to enjoy it more fully and in ways that will make our lives better in the long run.

But, even when we choose not to follow His instruction, His love for us doesn't change. Yes, we can have a better life if we follow God's commandments, but they don't affect His love for us. We get His perfect love no matter what we do.

LIVING IN LOVE: Choose God's love because of its perfect and unwavering nature, and then see if you aren't surprised by the ways you want to change how you live.

DAY 15
In Love There Is No Fear

For God has not given us a spirit of fear, but of power and of love and of a sound mind.

—2 Timothy 1:7

We've talked about the judgment, rejection, and torment that are part of our past experiences with love and how they skew our perception of God's love for us. It can be so hard to accept that God loves us because we are afraid He won't want someone like us—someone who is imperfect and makes mistakes. We let the fear of having the same experiences all over again keep us from knowing the kind of love God has to offer. We allow that fear to keep us from being able to show love as well.

But in God's perfect love there is no fear. We have the security of knowing His love is enduring. There is nothing that will make God stop loving us. We can take the risk of receiving and giving love because He won't criticize or humiliate us. He won't tell us we aren't good enough, smart enough, or pretty enough to be loved. Those things don't even enter into His love for us.

How comforting is it to realize that there is a love available to us so great and so deep that it eliminates all fear? And it isn't just the fears we have about being hurt in love that we can release. God's love covers a multitude of insecurities we have that keep us from blessings in life.

Our fear of not being enough is irrelevant because we are made whole in Him. The fear that we won't amount to anything in life is wiped out because He has placed an assignment on our lives that we will discover and fulfill when we are living in His love. When we fear for our financial and professional stability, we just have to turn to the promise He made in Philippians 4:19 that he will "supply all [our] need according to His riches in glory by Christ Jesus."

Our fear comes from not knowing what to expect or from having expectations that we think won't be met. We allow them to build up from our own past experiences and from the things we've observed in the lives of people around us. We let that fear grow until it consumes us and keeps us from being able to move out of the place where we are stuck. But, we will never have to doubt God's love or his intentions for our lives, and that gives us the freedom to grow and pour His love into the lives of others.

When you put on the love of God, you can be bold and strong. You can be brave and fearless. You can have the confidence to do all that He has called you to do without the fear of rejection or judgment.

LIVING IN LOVE: One by one, start releasing all the fears you carry around with you by focusing on the promises God made and the ways He empowers you to overcome those fears.

DAY 16
In Love There Is No Failure

For we have great joy and consolation in your love, because the hearts of the saints have been refreshed by you, brother.

—Philemon 1:7

We covered quite a few fears in the previous devotion, but we didn't touch on the fear of failure, and that's a big one. We miss out on so much in life simply by not even trying because we are afraid we won't do it well, that we will mess up, or that we will completely blow it. That kind of life is not a part of God's plan and definitely not part of His love.

We cannot fail when we are under the cover of God's perfect love. He will encourage and support us, instruct and guide us on the path He has laid out for us. He wants great things for us and loves us so much that He will do whatever it takes to see we get them.

When we are distracted from the mission, He will refocus our attention to where we are going. If we get tripped up along the way, He will pick us up, dust us off, and put us back on our way. For the times when we feel discouraged, He has given us His Word and places other people in our lives to help us find hope again. And, when we begin to wonder if this is worth it or if we are on the right track, He will show us the way, lighting our path so we are renewed in our determination. That is what His love does.

You've probably heard someone at some point say, "Failure is not an option." In some situations that can feel really intimidating instead of motivating because we don't see how we can succeed. We feel overwhelmed and lost and can't imagine how to get to the finish line. But God's love isn't about pushing you to the goal. He sees when you feel you can't keep going; and, instead of shouting at you like a drill sergeant, He whispers how much He loves you and shows you where to take the next step.

Failure is not an option in God's love, but not because He insists on it. It isn't an option because He won't let you down. He has blessings He wants to put on your life and if He needs you to be in a certain place or situation to receive them, He will work with you to make sure you get there.

In love there is no failure because God is working behind the scenes to make sure you succeed.

LIVING IN LOVE: When you are called to something in life, God is going to make sure you get there, so trust Him to guide your steps and your choices.

DAY 17
In Love There Is No Expiration Date

For I am persuaded that neither death nor life, nor angels nor principalities nor powers, nor things present nor things to come, nor height nor depth, nor any other created thing, shall be able to separate us from the love of God which is in Christ Jesus our Lord.

—Romans 8:38-39

The human mind has a hard time conceiving eternity. When we are teenagers, we can't even imagine being our parents' age. Try to imagine the amount of time that has passed since the world was created and how far that is going to stretch into the future. It is just too big to get our brains around. So, the thought of God loving us for that long without it ever changing is not something we can intellectually deal with. We have to take it into our hearts and process it spiritually.

Even when we take marriage vows and promise

to love someone until death do us part, we wonder if we can be consistent in it. We know there are going to be days when our spouse does that thing that really annoys us and we have a harder time saying, "I love you," and meaning it as much as we did on our wedding day. And, with divorce rates as high as they are, it can be easy to think it isn't possible to love someone for our entire lives.

In our humanity, that might be true. We certainly let it be true. But in God's perfect love there is no expiration date. There is no divorce or out clause. There is nothing that can separate us from His love, and that won't change. When we live in love and put on the love of God, we gain a better understanding of what this kind of love feels like and it enables us to begin showing that kind of love to others in our lives. If we truly know the kind of love God pours into us, it is a whole lot easier to love beyond the "use by" date we have put on our relationships and we are able to actually grow in love instead of running out of our supply or letting it dry up.

There is no way to wear out your welcome with God or come to the end of the love He has for you. Don't worry that there will come a day when He won't feel as strongly as He did when He created you. Even if you make choices or live in a way that disappoints Him, He won't check out on you. And even death will not terminate His love. In fact, He wants you to know His love so you can be with Him in eternity.

LIVING IN LOVE: Loving beyond the limitations of humanity is a God thing, but it is something we can have in our lives and something we can show others when we know Him.

DAY 18
In Love There Is Victory

What then shall we say to these things? If God is for us, who can be against us?

—Romans 8:31

When we come up against judgment and rejection, fear rears its ugly head making it hard for us to love. It becomes really easy to feel defeated by the experiences of our pasts and to want to give up. Each time we are wounded by someone and keep pulling back, we get more and more closed off from others and from God. And the enemy wins every time we choose not to give or receive love. But God is in our corner, and when we can realize what that means for us, we don't have to live with defeat.

In love there is victory, but it doesn't mean winning in the sense of beating someone in a contest—"I won the love of the girl I've been chasing," or "I'm the favorite kid and mom and dad love me best." That may be some kind of victory, but not a victory in love. If someone else loses in the process, it isn't really winning. The kind of victory I'm talking about and the kind that God wants for us in our lives is conquering the demons that keep us from feeling worthy of love, that prevent us from believing love can be unconditional, and that stop our progress toward living in the eternal love God has for us.

A victory in love is not about a game, competition, or race. It is about realizing that, no matter what you face in life, God is for you and will fight against any enemy to protect your best interests. But, ultimately, our victory is over death when we are living in the perfect love of God. That means when we come to the end of this life, we will not suffer the agony of separation from God because we have chosen to love Him and accept His love.

There are people, circumstances, and supernatural forces that would like to see us stay down in the fight and accept defeat. God wants us to get up and keep fighting. He wants us to remember that the love He is pouring into our lives is strong enough to overcome any opposition we will face because He's got our backs. Remember, there is no enemy who can stand against us when God is for us. That includes the enemy that hangs out in our minds too. When we are living in His love, He will help us knock down each negative, defeating message that comes up in our thoughts and replace them with messages of how much He wants for us.

God will deliver victory to us, helping us conquer anything that stands in the way of how He wants to love us, the hooked-up life He wants to give us, and the relationship He wants to have with us. You can claim that victory through His love.

LIVING IN LOVE: As you grow closer to God, you will begin to identify more and more enemies who would like to shut down your relationship with Him. That is when you lean into Him more closely and turn those battles over to Him.

DAY 19
In Love There Is Endurance

But in all things we commend ourselves as ministers of God...by purity, by knowledge, by longsuffering, by kindness, by the Holy Spirit, by sincere love....
—2 Corinthians 6:4&6

We talked about how there is no expiration date in love and how, as humans, it can be hard to comprehend a love that is eternal. We tend to have relationships that come and go. We usually feel love more strongly in the beginning—you know what that puppy love, honeymoon stage feels like. Everything is wonderful and magical. And then, later on, the romance starts to fade some. The little things that you thought were cute are now kind of annoying. Sometimes we let that lack of freshness affect us so much that we decide we don't feel love very strongly anymore and can actually let it fall apart. That's because we approach new love like a sprint, when our relationships should be treated like a marathon.

To be able to love the way God loves—whether it is romantic love, family love, friendship love—we have to come at it with the mindset of endurance. Now, I know everyone thinks they will love that person forever and that can't possibly change. And I'm sure that is their intent when they get started. But, oftentimes, we don't take the necessary steps in building the foundation for a love that can last that long.

There are lots of mistakes we make in the way we love on a human level. We try to overlook things that bother us, thinking we are loving unconditionally. The truth is we are just pretending they don't exist when we should be looking at them through the eyes of God and accepting every flaw and loving them anyway. Another mistake we make is how we avoid talking about what is on our hearts so we don't make the other person upset or angry because we are afraid they will reject us. We think giving in and getting along will help us avoid conflict. We think not having disagreements in our relationship is a good thing. But in a God-style love, we can talk about our concerns and show respect for one another to resolve those conflicts without hurting each other.

These are building blocks that set us up for endurance. Trusting God to strengthen our relationships and grow our love for one another is how love holds up over time. When we are living in love, we are in it for the long haul and don't look for excuses to quit; we don't allow anything to interfere with our love.

God has an enduring love for you that has no boundaries or limitations. It has been since the beginning of time and will remain. He is in this for eternity.

LIVING IN LOVE: When you put on the love of God, you start to treat love the way He does. Following Jesus' example is the best way to be a part of enduring love.

DAY 20
In Love There Is Faithfulness

Love never gives up, never loses faith, is always hopeful, and endures through every circumstance.

—1 Corinthians 13:7 NLT

The key to having a love that is strong and that endures all the trials we can face in life is faithfulness. Love that lasts will come up against hardships and trials over time. That's unavoidable. You will never have an entirely smooth ride in loving someone, so it is important to be dedicated to the journey. There is no love more faithful than the love God has for us. Even though we reject Him, disobey Him, question Him, and deny Him, His love remains just as secure and unchanging as it ever was.

Faithfulness is a big word that we really seem to struggle with a lot these days. I want you to look at it from two angles. Being faithful means being true to your commitments, but it also means being full of faith—having faith in something. The first meaning is usually associated with fidelity in a relationship. We are tempted everywhere we turn and it can feel nearly impossible to stay faithful sometimes, but it isn't just the temptation to cheat that challenges us. We can also be tested in how full of faith we are. We might be afraid that we aren't loved by that other person as much as we love them, and then the faith we have in that relationship is compromised. Other times we may question why we are loved and our confidence becomes shaken. When we doubt that we deserve love, we are not being faithful.

Faith is even harder to come by when we have had our trust violated by someone in the past. We allow those wounds to keep us from believing in the promises God has made to us; but, it is through His love and the promises He has kept that we can find the healing we need to be able to have faith again.

When we know the perfect love of God, all the

questions are answered, all the past is wiped away, all the fears are eliminated, and we are left with the pure and trustworthy love He is waiting to give to us. When we can have faith in that love, it allows us to be more loving and trusting with others. Being able to be filled with faith can only come from knowing God and feeling the depths of His love. Without that, we will continue to feel insecure and unwanted. It is only through His love that we can have the assurance that, through Jesus, we are guaranteed to experience a faithful love and a faith-filled life.

When you live in love, faithfulness becomes a natural extension of the love you are able to give and receive.

LIVING IN LOVE: As you put on the love of God, notice how your ability to have faith in love and to be faithful in love is strengthened each day.

Section 3

BECOMING LIMITLESS IN LOVE

DAY 21
In Love There Are No Conditions

Yet in all these things we are more than conquerors through Him who loved us.

—Romans 8:37

I've already mentioned how our belief that love is a works-based proposition keeps us from being able to accept that God's love doesn't come with rules and that we aren't going to experience rejection when we open up ourselves to that love. I want to make sure you understand that God's love is unconditional. That means he does not place any conditions on what way and when or how much love He gives out.

God is not going to say, "I love you as long as you do what I tell you to do," or "I will love you more if you can be good for this many days in a row." He is not going to give you less love because your neighbor gave a bigger offering at church or because someone else prayed a better prayer with fancier words. There are no conditions on His love.

I wonder sometimes if we really understand what the word *unconditional* means. We use it a lot, but we still can't seem to understand that God's love really is without condition. That is the only reason I can think of for why we wouldn't accept His love. Why else would we turn down the comfort, the blessings, and the assurances that come from His love except that we don't really get it?

God loves you because He does. There is no other reason or explanation. God loves you because He does. There isn't anything expected of you other than to let Him love you. God loves you because he does. You won't get a bill later with some hidden charges for His services or a termination letter because you didn't live up to your end of the bargain. God loves you because He does. He will not decide you aren't deserving because He needs more attractive people in Heaven. He just loves you.

These examples may sound ridiculous, but it is even more ridiculous to reject God's love when you have nothing to lose and everything to gain. You don't have to be perfect. You don't even have to be good. He is still going to love you. So, why would you not make the choice to start receiving that love immediately? It really is as unconditional as it gets.

LIVING IN LOVE: Even though it can be hard to believe that God doesn't place any conditions on loving us, the more you walk in His love, the more you will understand what that means and how limitless it really is.

DAY 22
In Love There Is No Cap

May [you] be able to comprehend with all the saints what is the width and length and depth and height—to know the love of Christ which passes knowledge; that you may be filled with all the fullness of God.
—Ephesians 3:18-19

Who doesn't like to be in a setting where the excitement is built up so much that it feels like it will lift the roof off the place? Maybe that's at a concert or a sports event. It could be at a party or even at church. That feeling is energizing and gets you all fired up for whatever you are a part of. This is how God feels about you every minute of every day. His love for you is so big that it is blowing the lid off.

Can you imagine what that is like? Are you getting that feeling now from your relationship with God? If not, you haven't really begun walking with Him and haven't put on His love. As Paul wrote in Ephesians, I want you to have the power to understand the scope of God's love. God's love stretches to the ends of the Earth because that is how wide He would search to find you and bring you back to Him. God's love reaches back to the beginning of time and stretches into eternity because that is how long He has loved you and will continue to love you. God's love goes beyond surface things like appearance, wealth, popularity, or behavior and gets right to the heart of who He made you to be because that is how deep His love runs. God's love opens up the gates of Heaven because that is how high He wants you to rise above the limits of your humanity.

There is no cap in love because it should reach infinitely into every direction. When we have put love on, it goes outward to those we find hard to love and inward to the parts of ourselves we thought were not deserving of love. God does not put a lid on His love to keep it from boiling over. He doesn't try to rein it in and keep it contained. He wants you to know how huge His love is so you can understand that it will never come up short and it will never run out. When you understand this, you can feel the freedom of allowing your love to overflow until it blows the roof off.

We have learned to be so guarded about giving out love, putting a cap on it, thinking, *I need to hold some back just in case I don't get anything in return*, or *I'd better make sure this doesn't get out of hand or I might drive people away.* If the worst thing people can say about you is that you loved too much or that you were so full of love that you couldn't hold it in, would that be so bad?

When you live in love, it becomes a part of everything you do and it spills out all over the place. There are things in life we should cap—hatred, greed, anger, violence—but love should never be in short supply.

Becoming Limitless in Love

LIVING IN LOVE: As you really embrace God's perfect love, you won't be afraid to let love flow freely. You can resist the need to put a cap on it because you will know you have access to an unlimited supply right from the source.

DAY 23
In Love There Are No Limits

And now abide faith, hope, love, these three; but the greatest of these is love.

—1 Corinthians 13:13

The verses in Chapter 13 of 1 Corinthians are the most well-known and often-quoted verses from the Bible on the topic of love. They lay out for us what love is, what it should look like, and why it is so important. Paul wrote about how we can have great speaking ability, the gift of prophecy, and understand all the mysteries of the world, but if we don't have love, we are nothing. We can have the faith to move mountains, give to the poor, and make personal sacrifices, but if we don't love, it means nothing.

If that doesn't confirm for you that God doesn't love us because of anything we can say or do, nothing will. Paul's letter to the Corinthians goes on to say,

"Love bears all things, believes all things, hopes all things, endures all things." (1 Corinthians 13:7) That means there are no limits in love. Love does not reach a breaking point where it can't take any more stress. It does not hit a wall from being tired and overwhelmed. Love does not reach a point of frustration and give up. We might experience those things in our humanity, and that's understandable, but love is the enduring thing that gets us through all of that.

The love God has for us will bring us to the other side and remind us of what is important. It will help us become renewed in our love and our strength to keep on pushing. With love we can get up and try again because love suffers long and it never fails. That definition of love has to be some of the most encouraging words God gives us in the Bible.

There are no limits to God's love, and there are no limits on what we can accomplish when we are living in love. In love, we do not envy others, we are not puffed up and arrogant, we are not rude or self-serving. We are not any of the things that limit the possibilities of love.

When we comprehend the kind of love God has for us, it opens us up to a limitless life that is free from restraints and full of restoration.

LIVING IN LOVE: Putting on love will allow you to move beyond the limits of the natural world and give meaning to everything you do with an eternal impact.

DAY 24
In Love There Are No Restrictions

But if you love those who love you, what credit is that to you? For even sinners love those who love them.
—Luke 6:32

The fear over rejection that prevents us from giving and receiving love comes from our past experiences with being restricted by others or placing restrictions on the love we give. We hold back, thinking that person who hurt us or betrayed us doesn't deserve to get our love. Sometimes we even choose not to love someone because we think they are hard to get along with or they take too much work.

These are restrictions we place on love that have no place there. We are reminded in Luke that we don't get credit for loving the ones who are easy to love. Everybody can do that. Why should you get points for loving your husband as long as he gives you what you want or for loving your kids when they are on their best behavior?

What about loving the smelly homeless man who sits outside your office entrance every day asking for help, the friend who betrayed your confidence, the business partner who embezzled and bankrupted your company, or the drunk driver who killed your sister? Those people are harder to love, but probably even more in need of it than anyone else in your life.

When you are able to find love in your heart to give to them, then you are loving with no restrictions. I have already reminded you several times that God's love has no limitations, no rules, no judgments, no expectations. It is important to repeat this message because it is so hard for us to understand. But, it is also necessary to keep driving it home because being able to take in that kind of love and extend it to others is even harder.

We are given unrestricted access to God's love even when we don't give that to the people in our lives who are hard to love. But, don't you think it would be a lot easier to understand how God can love us that way if we began practicing it ourselves? Wouldn't that kind of unrestricted love start to make more sense to us if we could try to love someone who hurt us and not just those who already love us?

Putting on love doesn't mean you have to allow those people to have access to your life in ways that could hurt you. It just means that you are able to show compassion, have forgiveness, and share God's love with them. When you are that covered in love it rubs off on everyone you come across, even the less desirable people in your world, and that is better for everyone.

LIVING IN LOVE: When you live in love, there are no more restrictions on who gets your love and how much of it they receive. You will find enough love for everyone.

DAY 25
In Love There Is Freedom

For you, brethren, have been called to liberty; only do not use liberty as an opportunity for the flesh, but through love serve one another.

—Galatians 5:13

I've talked a lot about the fears and obstacles that keep us from being able to comprehend God's love and show that kind of love to others. The greatest gift that comes from being able to put on love and walk in it is the freedom we experience once we get exactly what this love means.

We are free from being judged and from the need to judge others. We are free from the pain of rejection and don't have to reject others as a form of protection. We get to be free from the torment we put ourselves through by reliving past hurts. We are free from the rules, limitations, conditions, and restrictions. There is no more fear, no more failure. We are free to thrive and be victorious.

Is that not a life you want to be able to live? I can't imagine anyone choosing to remain in the bondage of fear and shame. Now, that does not mean we are free to go and live however we want. That is not what I am saying. You don't get a free pass to go live wild and loose and think, *God's going to forgive me, so I can do whatever I want.* You can't blackmail God with His own love. You don't get to say, "Well, God, you said you'd love me no matter what I do, so I'm gonna go do this and you have to forgive me and love me anyway." Even though God will forgive you and continue to love you, that is not what He meant, and that way of thinking is not a sign that you really understand the kind of love He is offering.

The freedom we are given is from binding thoughts, hurtful attitudes, and destructive behaviors. In love there is freedom from all of the parts of our humanity that keep us separated from God. When we can take that freedom and use it to thrive and grow and be able to spread the love of God everywhere we go, we are living in love.

Freedom is a gift that comes with some pretty big responsibility, but it is the key to being able to fully comprehend the love God has for you. Use the freedom you find in God's love to help you get rid of all of the baggage and negative messages once and for all. Let it open up your life to the blessings that come from being loved and being able to love freely.

LIVING IN LOVE: As you put on love, your understanding of what freedom really means will change. You can begin to view it as something that is not a pass to do whatever you want, but a key that will open doors to a closer relationship with God.

DAY 26
In Love There Is Abundance

And may the Lord make you increase and abound in love to one another and to all, just as we do to you.
—1 Thessalonians 3:12

Have you ever had a time when you felt so much love for someone that you would do anything for them? Especially when love is new and fresh, we can feel it through every part of our bodies. If you've had a child, you will remember what it felt like when they were born. You were completely caught up in your love for them. You couldn't stop looking at your son or daughter and just knew you would move heaven and earth for them. In fact, you were probably so full of love for your child that you loved everyone in your life even more.

That is the overflowing that Paul was writing to the church at Thessalonica about. The miraculous and wonderful thing about love is that when it fills you up until you are overflowing, it's not like with a water glass where what spills over is lost. When love is pouring into you at such a rate that you can't contain it all, it doesn't just fall on the floor and run into the cracks. It finds its way to the people around you. It spills over onto them and begins to fill their hearts until they are overflowing, and then the people around them are also affected in a positive way.

This is called abundance and it is what we find in God's perfect love. You may think that abundance refers to wealth, possessions, privilege, or influence. And, yes, when we are walking with God and receiving the fullness of His love, there are blessings—what I like to call the hooked-up life—that are part of what God has planned for you and they can come in the form of worldly possessions. But, if you focus on that, you are limiting God because abundance is really about making room for God to work in your life. When you do that, He is able to change your heart so you can align with His will for you. He can give you freedom from the behaviors and attitudes that keep you from succeeding or even believing you deserve to have success. He will lift the fear that prevents you from being bold enough to step into His promises for a better life. He will release you from the bondage of addictions that keep you trapped in a cycle that hurts you, your family, and Him.

There is abundance in love that will overflow into every part of your life when you are walking with God and putting on the love He has for you.

LIVING IN LOVE: When you live in love, you won't be concerned about letting your love flow abundantly because you have the confidence that it will return to you in even greater abundance.

DAY 27
In Love There Is Forgiveness

And he arose and came to his father. But when he was still a great way off, his father saw him and had compassion, and ran and fell on his neck and kissed him.

—Luke 15:20

Even those who never went to Sunday school as children know this story of the Prodigal Son. It is a perfect illustration of the way God loves us and of the forgiveness He will give to us over and over because of His perfect love. We probably struggle more with the concept of forgiveness than any other aspect of life and being able to love. It is nearly impossible for us to comprehend how God can forgive some of the things we do and that when He does, they are completely gone and forgotten. We have an even harder time trying to figure out how to forgive ourselves and others who hurt us.

In our relationships, we are called to forgive what is done to us as many times as are necessary. One of our biggest issues with this instruction is being okay with forgiving repeatedly. We ask, *If I keep forgiving them, won't they keep doing it? Why should I let that happen?* Or we might wonder, *Do I have to forgive someone who hasn't asked for forgiveness?* The answer to all of these questions is that we aren't asked to forgive people to benefit them or to make them feel better. God wants us to forgive because when we hold onto anger, bitterness, and resentment it interferes with our ability to love and it keeps us disconnected from Him. Forgiveness releases all of the emotions and thoughts that keep us stuck in the past.

Whether we are trying to deal with ourselves for mistakes we have made that may have hurt ourselves or other people or if we are confronting others who have hurt us in some way, without forgiveness we will not be able to receive all that God wants to pour into our lives. We will be too distracted by the negative feelings we are holding onto and will miss what God is saying to us.

When we are unable to forgive, it makes it much harder to believe that God really forgives us. We think He is probably keeping a ledger of everything we did wrong somewhere so that, when we mess up the next time, He can pull it out and add it to the total. It is not possible to accept that we are totally forgiven when we aren't able to give that to ourselves or to the people who are in need of our forgiveness.

In God's perfect love we find complete forgiveness and the ability to forgive as well. It is one of the hardest lessons, but also one of the most rewarding.

LIVING IN LOVE: In order to put on love, you have to remove the anger and bitterness that come from not forgiving. As you walk in love, and you accept God's forgiveness, forgiving yourself and others will become easier.

DAY 28
In Love There Is Sacrifice

Greater love has no one than this, than to lay down one's life for his friends.

—John 15:13

This verse in John says that there is no greater love than laying down your life for another. That is the ultimate sacrifice—the same one that Jesus made for us. Thankfully, most of us will not ever be asked to make a sacrifice that big, but there will be other things asked of us as a part of giving and receiving love that can feel almost as difficult.

"Sacrifice" just sounds like an unreasonable thing to ask. We might have to sacrifice a small portion of our money to help someone in need. We could have to sacrifice some of our free time to support the interests of someone in our family. We may need to sacrifice a little pride to say I'm sorry, even when we don't think we did anything wrong, so we can have peace. Those should not seem like a big deal, but when we are not walking in love, they can have a big effect on our attitudes.

So, imagine what it will feel like when we are asked to make an even bigger sacrifice and aren't operating from a perspective of love. How would you handle having to give up a job you love so you can take care of an elderly parent with a serious illness? What will you do when you have to leave your friends and your home and move to another state because your spouse was transferred?

There are going to be times in life when we have to make choices that cost us something important because it is in someone else's best interests. Those decisions can make or break our relationships if we are not walking in love as we make them. We can let resentment build up until we are so angry it affects the way we treat the people in our lives.

Love is the greatest thing we have in life, but it can

involve really hard choices. And, making sacrifices is one of the most loving things you can do. The sacrifice Jesus made was the greatest expression of love we will ever see. But, even when it isn't an easy choice, the reward that comes from putting someone else before yourself is greater than anything you might have to give up.

When you put on love, it does not make sacrifice easy or pain-free; it just makes the choice clear and helps you realize why it is necessary.

LIVING IN LOVE: As you draw closer to God and rely on His love in tough times, you will find the courage to make sacrifices for those who need you.

DAY 29
In Love There Is Humility

Now before the Feast of the Passover, when Jesus knew that His hour had come that He should depart from this world to the Father, having loved His own who were in the world, He loved them to the end.

—John 13:1

The example Jesus sets for us shows us how to love in every situation where we might find ourselves. He shows us the limitless nature of love, the abundance and forgiveness we can expect from love, and the sacrifice that is a necessary part of love. As we are growing in His love and discovering all of the good things we are doing for others through that love, it can be easy to get a little full of ourselves.

In our humanity, we can forget that the God-sized love that is flowing through us doesn't come from our own ability. Without God—without knowing Him and the depth of His love—we would not be capable of loving this way. This is when we need to remember another trait of Jesus' love: humility. Jesus was the absolute definition and manifestation of love, but He did not boast about it or brag that He was better than anyone. Jesus didn't go around reminding everyone of all the good deeds He did in a day. He didn't keep a scorecard of all the times He forgave with stars for the "big" sins He let slide.

Jesus was humble, and even though He claimed the power that came from God's love in Him, He gave the glory to God. This is the way we are supposed to live in love. When we put on God's love and walk in it, we are not supposed to parade around like we are wearing some Olympic medal. Every action we take out of love should be with an attitude of service and humility.

Jesus loves us and loves serving us. He wants to help meet our needs and bless us. We should have that same attitude when we share His love with everyone we meet. Part of loving the way God loves us is the relentless pursuit of relationship with those we love. When you are so desperate to give love, it is really hard to be prideful about it.

When Jesus knew His time had come to return to His father in Heaven, He didn't try to stay and be the king they were asking Him to be. He could have let them worship Him as they wanted to do, but He knew His time on Earth was finished, and He had a final expression of love to make in order to fulfill His purpose. He didn't go out in a blaze of glory. He humbly died knowing many would not get why he had to go and others would mock Him.

Understanding God's love means accepting that we won't always get credit for the things He calls us to do to show His love.

LIVING IN LOVE: As you begin living in God's love, you will grow to value self less and less. You can begin to show His love in ways that focus on the other person's needs and glorifying God.

DAY 30
In Love There Is Unity

But above all these things put on love, which is the bond of perfection.

—Colossians 3:14

One of the bigger problems people have with comprehending God's love and wanting to have that in their lives is the way Christians advertise it. Oftentimes, we come at them with our arsenal of reasons for why they need God in their lives and they end up feeling judged and attacked instead of loved and wanted.

Have you ever met anyone who was convinced to come to church and ended up thriving and growing and choosing God through an encounter with a hater? We have to get out of the mode of going on the defensive trying to make an argument for why they need God's love like it is a criminal case. I have never heard anyone say that being told they were a terrible person and their life was a wreck made them want to buy what that person was selling.

We have to be more sensitive to the spirit so God can reveal to us how to minister in love to others—showing them instead of telling them. When we use our actions instead of our words to demonstrate what God can do in their lives, it says way more than any speech could. The way we treat people will either drive them away or draw them closer. God's love is unifying and should never be something that divides people.

As it says in Colossians that love is the fabric that binds us together in harmony. It unites us with a common purpose—to love one another. When we put on love, our focus is to bring people together so we can accomplish great things through Jesus and spread His love everywhere. There are so many people who live in darkness and hopelessness because they don't know the perfect love of God. When we are unified in God's love, we can accomplish anything. There are so many things people suffer in life that we could resolve if we worked together.

Being united is an expression of love and it requires love. There is no room for egos or personal agendas when you are working together for a common goal. Individual interests have to be checked at the door.

Love is the best way to unite people no matter what background, perspectives, or experiences they come from. It overcomes every boundary, limitation, or judgment that stands in the way of people coming together to do something good.

LIVING IN LOVE: When you walk with God in love, your desire to unite people grows. You can find ways to work around any obstacle that might prevent harmony when you come at it from a place of love.

Section 4

LIVING IN LOVE

DAY 31
In Love There Is Fullness

No one has seen God at any time. If we love one another, God abides in us, and His love has been perfected in us.

—1 John 4:12

Probably the saddest thing I see in ministry is people who are wounded and feel empty because they don't feel loved. The ways this shows up in their lives can be really destructive. Most of the behaviors that lead to addiction, abuse, and low self-esteem start because someone feels unloved and unworthy. And, that kind of pain doesn't have to happen.

We have the opportunity to show others the complete, unconditional, eternal love of God through the way we talk, the way we act, and the way we live out the love we receive from Him. There is not a single thing in our lives that can't be improved by approaching it with God's perfect love. Whether we are talking about poverty, disease, crime, hatred, or any other problems that keep us from living a rich and full life, it all starts with giving and receiving love.

When we don't feel loved, we don't have the confidence to reach for our full potential. We might feel trapped on a path that doesn't use the gifts God gave us. We might fall into bad relationships because we don't think we deserve anything better. We might allow temptations to creep into our lives and lead us into harmful behaviors because we don't think anyone cares what happens to us. Sometimes we end up in bad situations all because we are looking for love but don't know the right places to look for it. The bottom line is that we settle for less because we don't think we can have the greatness of God's love.

All the answers we need are found in the love God wants to give us. In Him, the holes we were trying to fill will be overflowing. Every self-esteem issue and unhealed wound will be gone when we learn just how great and how full His love is. When we learn to walk in love, we can wipe out all of the things that kept us feeling empty, and we can begin to pour that same love into the people around us.

Paul's letter to Timothy tells him not to let anyone think less of him because he is young, because in Christ he is more than that one thing. I encourage you to know the same kind of fullness in Christ. You are not "less than" in any way or for any reason when you are walking in Him.

LIVING IN LOVE: As you discover the fullness of God's love, you will begin to see all your life can be and all the ways you can pour life-changing love into others.

DAY 32
In Love There Is Sharing

So, affectionately longing for you, we were well pleased to impart to you not only the gospel of God, but also our own lives, because you had become dear to us.

—1 Thessalonians 2:8

When we experience the fullness that is in God's love, the first thing most of us want to do is start sharing it with others. The love we get from Him is so big that we can't help but be overflowing with it. But that only happens once we comprehend how much He loves us. And, until we have a genuine encounter with God's love, there is no way to fully understand or be able to share it. I didn't just wake up one day tired of dealing with my drug addiction and decide I was done with it. It wasn't until I had an encounter with Jesus Christ that I even knew I could live differently, much less really start changing.

On my way to buy more drugs, Jesus stepped into my life and showed me how much He loved me in a way I couldn't ignore, and I had no choice but to respond. The night I gave my life to Jesus, I immediately started telling everyone I came across. I went out to find the people who mattered most to me so I could tell them, because when you know how great it is to have that kind of love, you can't keep it to yourself. You have to start sharing it. I was sure people would want it. I knew they needed it as much as I did.

Oftentimes, we let our past experiences affect our understanding of God's love and our ability to give love. We think God couldn't possibly love us because we have done this or that to disqualify us from love or we think all love is going to end badly because of the way we have been treated by others. What has happened is that we have not had a true encounter with God's love yet, and it is not likely that the people in our lives who made us feel this way about love have had an encounter either. To know God is to know love, so when you finally get it—when you can finally comprehend His perfect love—something changes in you. The deep love you feel is something you just have to share because you want everyone to know about it and that God-sized love is more than you can contain inside of you.

When we put on love and walk with God, we have something that we need to share—and we are even called to share it—with the world. Responding to that urging is what it means to live in love.

LIVING IN LOVE: As God's love fills you, it isn't the kind of thing you want to keep to yourself. As you grow in that love, don't fight the urge that will build up in you to spread it around.

DAY 33
In Love There Is Acceptance

Beloved, let us love one another, for love is of God; and everyone who loves is born of God and knows God.

—1 John 4:7

We talked about how the fear of rejection and the expectation of rejection keeps us from being open to love and stands in the way of our ability to comprehend God's love. But the true nature of God's love is complete acceptance. It doesn't matter where you come from or what you have done in your past; it doesn't even matter where you go or what you do in your future. God is going to love you regardless.

You may say, "Oh, but you don't know me. You don't know what I've done. I have done things that are unforgiveable, and I don't deserve love." I may not know what sins you've committed in your past or what is in your heart right now, but I do know that if you think any of it matters to God, then you don't know Him. I can also tell you that God *does* know every bit of your past and your future and He loves you anyway.

God is going to accept you into His arms and hold on to you for dear life. He wants you with Him. He wants you to receive His love and to get to know Him. He doesn't care about any of the things that you think make you unlovable. Now, that doesn't mean he doesn't care about how you act, how you treat others, or how you treat yourself. He does. A lot. But, His concern for the condition of your heart and your soul does not affect His ability to love you. In fact, it is because He has so much love for you that He wants the best for you and wants to see you avoid the things that are harmful and damaging to your life.

God may not accept some of the choices you make as being good for you, but He still accepts you. When you understand that, it helps you to change how you choose to live your life and it changes the way you are with others. Once you are able to walk in love, there won't ever be another question of whether you are accepted and loved because you will feel God's presence every step of the way.

Being wanted and accepted is something we all need, and when we feel like an outcast, it affects our perception of ourselves and of God. Thankfully, when we live in love, the acceptance becomes a two-way street where we finally accept what God has made available to us all along.

LIVING IN LOVE: When you are living in love, you will be able to shed the old feelings of rejection and unworthiness that kept you from accepting God's love.

DAY 34
In Love There Is Confidence

Love has been perfected among us in this: that we may have boldness in the day of judgment; because as He is, so are we in this world.

—1 John 4:17

Being afraid of rules and judgment can affect how we perceive God's love. One of the reasons it can be so hard to believe God would love us in the state we are in is that we have no confidence in how or why He made us. We don't understand that God gave us life because He wants a relationship with us.

You might find it really hard to trust that there is anything about you that He could love, especially if you are used to hearing about all of your faults from someone who was supposed to love you. And, if all you've ever heard of God is all the Dos and Don'ts He gives out, you may think you don't want to have any part of that.

While God does not like sin, when He looks at you that is not what He sees. He sees His creation—the person He made out of complete love, the person He designed with a purpose—that He wants to draw closer to Him. Since God made us to love us, and since He loves us just because He does, you can have confidence in the fact that there is nothing you can do or say to change His love for you. You can have confidence in His intention to guide you and help you grow in Him.

In our humanity, our confidence can be easily shaken. We can be so fragile that a negative comment from one person can destroy the self-esteem we worked so hard to build up. You could be accomplished in every area of your life—getting good grades in school, having a successful career, keeping plenty of money in the bank—but still not feel confident because you don't feel loved.

The amazing thing about God's love is that we are all the same in His eyes. We are all special in His eyes and all loved by Him the same. That means we can be confident that His love doesn't play favorites and that it endures no matter what changes in our lives. And, as we grow closer to Him, the more confidence we will have that His promises are true.

As 1 John 4:17 says, when we live in Him, our love—our ability to love and comprehend God's love—grows more perfect. That means we gain confidence in the truth of His love and we gain confidence in who we are as children of God. That is what it means to put on love.

LIVING IN LOVE: As we live in love, we let go of our egos and gain true confidence in God and in who God made us to be. This changes the way we are able to love Him as well as the people around us.

DAY 35
In Love There Is Passion

Be kindly affectionate to one another with brotherly love, in honor giving preference to one another.

—Romans 12:10

Passion is oftentimes just associated with romantic love, but passion is really any strong feeling that makes you enthusiastic or excited. When we grow in God's love and really come to know Him, our passion for Him is ignited. We start to get passionate about telling others about God's love.

Some of the most enthusiastic people you will ever meet in your life are the ones who have just had an encounter with Jesus Christ. The passion that burns in them is like nothing you will feel at any other time in your life—not even the first time you fall madly and deeply in love—because of the way it fills you up; you can't get that kind of love from anywhere else.

Sometimes we can let that passion die down because we are human and we forget to keep walking with God through each day. We may accept God's love, but we don't actually put it on and wear it. That is where the passion comes from—living in love and letting it become central to your life.

We should never let our passion for God die down because we can be sure His passion for us never lessens. He is all about us, constantly seeking a relationship, wanting to be close to us. In fact, He is so passionate about us that He created humanity so we would exist for Him to love us. How is that for enthusiasm?

And it doesn't stop there. God gets so excited about us that He is working in our lives every day to make sure we have access to what we need, and He is just waiting for us to get passionate about Him so He can do amazing things in us and through us.

When we stay close to God, we can feel His passion and are able to know His will for our lives. And that gives us the fire to go out and love others and show them how important they are to God as well.

Walking in love keeps the passion alive in your relationship with God because you are drawing closer and closer to Him, fueling the fire.

LIVING IN LOVE: Passion isn't just for romance, and it is necessary for keeping us focused on sharing God's love with everyone who needs to know Him. Living in Love means keeping that passion alive.

DAY 36
In Love There Is Purity of Heart

Let no one despise your youth, but be an example to the believers in word, in conduct, in love, in spirit, in faith, in purity.

—1 Timothy 4:12

The Bible says anyone who do not love does not know God, and it also says they will know us by our love, meaning they will know we are Christians—aligned with God—by the way we love. In this verse where Paul is writing to Timothy, he instructs him that he is to be an example in the way he lives, the way he loves, the way he demonstrates his faith, and in his purity.

Paul is telling Timothy that the way to show others what God's love is doing in his life is by using his life as proof. He talks about Timothy's purity. One of the things about our youth that we admire when we are looking back to the past is that aspect of being a child when we are pure. We don't have any judgments or pre-conceived ideas about people. We don't have any agendas and aren't into manipulating people to see what we can take from them. When we are young, we don't let fear keep us from doing things that might be out of the box, and we aren't eaten up with worry.

When we put on God's love and we are able to rest in the knowledge that He loves us unconditionally, we can get back to the place where our hearts are pure and we don't have concerns about what we need to do to keep deserving love or what others have to do to earn our love. We can love purely and perfectly the way God loves us.

Even when our lives aren't pure and we are stuck in sin, God loves us and He wants to draw us closer to him so we can begin to set our hearts and minds right. But we don't have to be free of sin for God to love us. He is able and He is willing to work with us to purify us after we come to Him. In fact, the only way we really can become pure is to come to Him first and let Him love and restore us.

The purity of heart we have as children is a lot like how we feel when we begin to walk in God's love. When we put that on and let God fill our hearts, we are able to go back to the kind of love we were able to have as children, but on a deeper and more transformative level.

The purity of heart that comes from knowing God's love means casting off all of the experiences of the past and embracing a new way of living and loving.

LIVING IN LOVE: As we learn how to live in love, God cleanses our hearts and minds and fills us with hope and promise that we can pour into the lives of others who need to know His love as well.

DAY 37
In Love There Is Transformation

For the love of Christ compels us, because we judge thus: that if One died for all, then all died.

—2 Corinthians 5:14

As we walk in love and draw closer to God, we learn that we are loved unconditionally and that there is nothing that will stand in the way of His love or change His love for us. The one thing that will change is us. When we begin to feel the love of God filling our hearts and our lives, things begin to shift in our attitudes and our thinking. We take on a new way of being that models Jesus more closely. We become capable of love without judgment or expectation, just as He is. We want different things from life and our focus is on honoring and pleasing God instead of on serving our own interests.

Putting on love makes us different. We experience

a transformation in our lives and begin to understand things in a spiritual sense that we could not have comprehended in the natural. We start to get what it means to live in God and we modify the way we behave to embrace His will for our lives. All of the worldly influences that used to direct our choices are replaced by a deep desire to honor God and love like Him.

Transformation is not just acting a different way or dressing a different way. It goes so much deeper than changing your language or the people you associate with. Transformation is about a complete shift in how you view love and how you feel about giving and receiving it. Transformation happens at the very core of our being, and it doesn't just put a bandage on the wounds of our pasts; it heals them and makes us whole again. The transformational power of God's love is greater than anything else we might experience because it helps us overcome even the most intense strongholds on our lives.

When we put on God's love, we receive strength

to walk away from addiction and other destructive behaviors, we have the confidence we need to take on any challenge, and we are filled with the assurance to let go of all of the past experiences that affect how we give and receive love.

The transformation that comes from God's love allows us to live in love, no matter what we face.

LIVING IN LOVE: When we experience the transformation that happens as we walk in love, our lives are changed and we can begin to change the lives of others in a positive way as well.

DAY 38
In Love There Is More

And this I pray, that your love may abound still more and more in knowledge and all discernment..."

—Philippians 1:9

Sometimes when I tell someone "God loves you," the response I get is less than enthusiastic. They might scoff at me or say something along the lines of, *Well, that's nice, preacher. I appreciate it; but what's the big deal really? What good does that really do me?* This is a sign that they have not had a true encounter with Jesus to be able to comprehend God's love. They are probably comparing it to all the other times someone told them "I love you" and thinking about how that never amounted to much or didn't make a difference in their lives in a good way.

Some of them might even think that when someone says, "I love you," it means they now expect something in return. Maybe they were in a relationship where love was equated with gifts or sex. Maybe they heard the word love but were mistreated or ignored. These people have no concept of what real, perfect love could do for them. They don't have a clue of what this God kind of love holds for them. This is why it is important for us to put on that love and walk around in it, so they can begin to see how much more there is to love than nice feelings and affection.

The first thing we discover is that in God's love there is more love. There is more love to share; there is an abundance of room for giving and receiving love. As we dig deeper and draw closer to Him, we find there is more understanding of who He is and what He is all about. As we peel away the layers, we get closer and closer to knowing Him and the plans He has for us. There is so much God wants for us in life, and when we are not living in His love, we are settling for less than what God intends for us. We are missing out on more peace, more comfort, more joy, more confidence, more acceptance, and more passion in our lives. God pours things into us that we cannot access on our own. So, when we think we can get along fine without Him, we are short-changing ourselves and everyone else in our lives.

God has an abundant life set aside just for you, but in order to receive it, you have to receive His love and walk with Him. Don't let a misconception of what God's love holds keep you from experiencing the kind of life that can be so much more.

LIVING IN LOVE: Living in love requires more of you because you can't just receive and receive without giving too; but, the more you receive, the more you have to give so you don't come up short.

DAY 39
In Love There Is Strength

"Then Christ will make his home in your hearts as you trust in him. Your roots will grow down into God's love and keep you strong."

—Ephesians 3:17 [NLT]

The experiences of our pasts often affect how we perceive love and how we perceive ourselves. We can feel undeserving of love and unable to love because of these negative messages that skew our perspective. This weakens our ability to stand up for ourselves and insist that someone treat us right. It makes us vulnerable and susceptible to being misled. We all have things in our lives that keep us from being strong in our faith and our convictions—struggles that impact the choices we make.

The lack of love we can endure in our lives strips us of the strength that keeps us confident in who we are when we don't know all that God wants to offer us as His creations. It also robs us of the assurance that love is enduring and can overcome any obstacles.

When we put on God's love, we begin to understand the power that comes from loving the way He does and allowing ourselves to be loved by Him. I never would have had the personal strength to overcome my addictions without first having an encounter with God where I felt his love enter every part of me. Paul writes to the Ephesians about Christ making His home in our hearts. And that is how we are able to grow in strength—when we let Him work on us from the inside and change our hearts. He gives us His strength to endure and to rise up against challenges and temptations.

In our humanity, the things we experience in life can really tear us down and keep us frustrated and overwhelmed. That is not the way God wants us to live. He wants us to feel empowered by Him to overcome the hardships and the disappointments and the emotional scars so we can be strong for others. When you find strength in Him, you have what it takes to pull others up out of their places of hopelessness and helplessness.

There is strength in love, enough to move mountains and to change the world. As we walk with God, He will build us up so we can make a difference in the lives of everyone we meet.

LIVING IN LOVE: Living in love is living with God in your heart so He is with you, pouring His love and His strength into you for everything you face in life. When you go around with that kind of power, you can't help but change lives.

DAY 40
In Love There Is Everything

And do everything with love.

—1 Cor. 16:14 [NLT]

Paul's instruction in his letter to the Corinthians was to do everything with love. That is a message directly from God because that is how He wants us to live. He showed us through the example of Jesus that love should be the starting point for everything we do, it should be at the center of everything we do, and it should be the way we finish everything we do.

We have gone through a long list of reasons why we need God's love in our hearts and discussed all the obstacles that keep us from embracing His love. I've explained the different aspects of love that make our lives richer and better. And we've also covered what it looks like to live in love and how that affects our lives and the lives of others. All of it comes down to this very simple principle: Do everything in love and you can't go wrong. When you do, you will discover how love changes you and your thinking. It removes all the pain and disappointment of the past and opens you up to a more hopeful future.

When we do everything in love, everything changes. When we put on love, that becomes our way of handling everything and everyone we encounter; and in God's love we find everything we need to grow and become who He wants us to be. Everything we will do or experience in life is affected by the presence or lack of love, and when God's love is in the mix, it goes to a whole other level.

The journey we are on in our lives is for the purpose of growing in Him, learning to understand Him, and discovering the depth, width, height, and length of His love so we can embrace it and share it with others. We are called to put on His love and wear it around with us wherever we go so that we can make it a part of everything we do. He wants us to walk with Him and abide in Him so love is accessible in every moment. We will come to want to live in love because everything in life is better when we keep love at the center.

Doing everything with love isn't always easy, but it always results in something rewarding and enriching.

LIVING IN LOVE: As you live in love, it will become a habit to do everything with love. You will never regret putting love at the center of your life.

Closing Note from Jay

Finally, all of you be of one mind, having compassion for one another; love as brothers, be tenderhearted, be courteous . . .

— 1 Peter 3:8

God has immeasurable and enduring love that He wants to pour into our lives, but it can only be manifested in our lives if we commit to spending time in His Word. We have to immerse ourselves in His Word to fully understand what His love brings to us and to be able to accept that love and really take it in.

The love He gives us is something we are intended to share with others, and in doing that we can join together to grow in His love and become one, as His people. There are so many things out in the world competing for your attention and your devotion. If you don't get into the Word and surround yourself with others who are like-minded, those other influences can grab hold of you and pull you away from God and everything He wants to pour into your life.

Relationships take work, and if you don't keep at it, the relationship will fall into trouble. The same is true in our relationship with God. That is why I encourage you to keep digging deeper into what His word says about love and every other aspect of your lives where you need guidance and support.

God is waiting to love you. He wants to walk with you and share your life with you. When you take the steps to begin living in love, you will begin living with God as well. Put on God's love and make Him an intimate part of your life.

In God's love,
Pastor Jay

THE SANCTUARY

What God is doing in The Sanctuary is so extraordinary. His presence shows up here and those who attend are saved, delivered, set free, and filled with the awesome power of the Holy Spirit. God's miracles happen here on a regular basis and lives are extremely, consistently, eternally being changed. I love our church! It is incredible! We would love for you to join us and receive from God in this amazing atmosphere!

We are a REAL church for REAL people. In fact, the word R.E.A.L. sums up our vision.

- R is for Reaching.
- E is for Equipping.
- A is for Aligning.
- L is for Legacy.

All of our ministries, in fact, everything we do, lines up with this vision.

"Come be a part! Get plugged into one of our ministries! Let's build God's Kingdom together!"

Our Worship Ministry is an integral part of what our church is all about. We are definitely an impassioned church, pursuing God, vertically focused in all our services. We've done everything we've done, faithfully, to get to where we are now as a church: The Sanctuary World Outreach. It seems like this is only just the starting point for us. We are on our way to planting churches in major cities of the world. To say I'm excited about our future is a major understatement.